Contents

High heels – or string vests?

Bill Bright's flight has just landed in High Springs, America.

But there is a slight problem – all the bags have got mixed up!

Help Bill and the rest of the passengers to get the right bag.

The passengers are:

Bill Bright (on a fishing trip)

Wayne Wightman (ten, visiting his penpal)

Coleen Highsmith (sixteen, on holiday)

Anna Knight (a mum with three kids, visiting her dad)

Fred Gray (an old man, off to see the big fight between Lightning Len and Mighty Mick)

Arabella Pecksniff–Wright (a frightfully posh lady, off to a frightfully posh wedding; just call her Your Highness!)

Bill Bright has got a light pink bag (very posh).

Contents:

- a fan
- a box of chocs
- high heels
- a long red dress with black spots
- silk stockings
- a posh pink hat
- fifteen gold rings
- a flight mask
- a tin of pins
- a wedding present (a green glass dish, wrapped up)
- six silk tops
- a packet of mints

Who gets this bag?

Wayne Wightman has got a scruffy black bag.

Contents:

- a stick
- teeth (in a box)
- a green check tweed cap
- three string vests
- a bag of toffees
- three currant buns
- a jam sandwich
- glasses (in a box)
- socks with clocks on
- 'Boxing – all the best fights'

Who gets this bag?

Coleen Highsmith has got a black rucksack.

Contents:

- a ball
- socks
- swimming trunks
- a swimming cap
- a green sun hat
- ten packs of gum
- DVDs
- lots of sweets
- three bags of crisps
- six bags of nuts
- an MP3 player

Who gets this bag?

Anna Knight has got a bright green bag.

Contents:

- vests
- pants
- thick socks
- fishing rods
- a tin of maggots
- black wellingtons
- a map of all the ponds in High Springs

Who gets this bag?

Fred Gray has got a bright green bag – this one has a lucky teddy on it!

Contents:

- sunglasses
- flipflops
- pink fluffy slippers
- tights
- a frilly nightdress
- fifteen dresses
- lots of bright strappy tops
- black leggings
- a pink belt
- a laptop
- an MP3 player
- a pink teddy
- suntan stuff

Who gets this bag?

Arabella Pecksniff-Wright has got a red bag on wheels.

Contents:

- a nightdress
- cheese and ham sandwiches in a plastic box
- three plastic cups
- a box of rusks
- a teddy
- lots of baby stuff
- three dolls
- three bibs with green sheep on them
- baby milk

Who gets this bag?

Have they all got the right bag?

Know your fright limit!

Own up! What gives you the creeps?

Do this "fright check" quiz to show the true you ...

gutsy or gutted? Check your fright limit!

Set-up 1

In bed at night. You spot a shadow you did not expect to see.

You think:

a) That's a bit odd. Not keen on that, but I'm sleepy so I'll just shut my eyes and nod off ...

F.L. (Fright Limit)

b) Shadow? At night? I don't wish to think what it is! Heck – I think it's growing! Put the light on! Muuuuuuuuum!

F.L.

c) Hmmm ... big shadow by the window tonight. Did shadows in science last week. It's just an object backlit on to, say, a wall.

F.L.

Set-up 2

You are staying at Gran's bungalow in the holidays.

The creepiest thing you see is ...

a) An old chest in the hall. You think it might have a body in it! Gran will not say what is in that chest ...
(Who was bumped off in the bungalow?)

F.L.

b) The list of jobs Gran has for you to do tomorrow. Mow grass, polish windows, throw away the rubbish in the shed, peel the spuds, weed between rows of veg she grows ...

F.L.

c) Gran's teeth in a glass by her bed.

F.L.

EEEEEEK!!

Set-up 3

It's fright night on TV. You are chilling with your pals and a film showing little green men visiting from Planet Zog has just ended. You nip to the kitchen where fizzy pop and crisps are stowed away. Standing by the window you spot a little man on the grass! You ...

a) Think, "Mum did say the grass needs mowing. Must have got that man from number 24 to do it."

F.L. (1 ghost)

b) Swallow a crisp and yell, "Okay! Which one of you is showing off your acting skills (not)? Hello? It is one of you ... isn't it?"

F.L. (2 ghosts)

c) Throw the crisps! Drop the pop! Squeeze in the narrow bit below the sink and bellow for help!

F.L. (4 ghosts)

Fright Limit tot up:

Below 3 = top fright limit. Not much gives you the creeps. You just go with the flow!

3 – 6 = middle to high fright limit. Impressive. Frightened, but you don't show it.

7 – 10 = low fright limit. Yellow belly!

Do you do zoos?

If you visit a zoo, you might have mixed feelings when you see the animals on show. Are zoos a good thing? A bad thing? Does it seem wrong that the animals cannot run free, or do you think it is good that they get food and are well looked after? Look at what Jools and Jay have to say on the subject …

This is Jools and Jools knows what she thinks! Go, Jools!

Look at it this way – if I was an animal (from a baboon to a kangaroo), I'd choose to live in a zoo with lots of good grub and a keeper checking I'm okay from noon until night! Bliss!

It is cool to go on a trip to a zoo. Okay – I know zoos can smell a bit, but what is wrong with a bit of a pong when you get to see an elephant! (Right – that will be a big pong …)

Zoos are brilliant! Lots of animals might be extinct if zoos did not breed them.

Meet Jay. He *so* disagrees with Jools on zoos. Say it, Jay!

Animals in zoos have to put up with hundreds of kids, mums and dads trooping in to look at them. Not cool!

No fooling. Zoos are not good! What a way to live, spending days on end cooped up in a pen with no freedom to run, stretch and hunt your own food!

Zoos say they breed animals that might soon be extinct, but lots of animals do not breed well in captivity. They need the right habitat. Animals can be helped to breed in their own habitats.

Who is right?
Jools? Jay?
What might an animal have to say?

Orang-utan 1

Orang-utan fenced in a pen,
drenched in a grey light.
She clings and swings
on swaying, rubber rings.

Plucks at grub
in a plastic tray –
zoo food left
there day after day.

Sits, hunched, in a paddock
on patches of grass,
grooming her dull, grizzled fur
as it catches the light of a grey, drizzle mist.

Orang-utan 2

Orang-utan in a tropical forest,
drenched in a cool, green light.
She clings and swings
on swaying limbs
of trees.

Plucks at grubs,
feeds and sleeps
high in a vast,
ripped umbrella
roof of branches.

Her mad, matted fur
catches wet drops
of light as they pelt
to the bottom
of a lush, growing world.

Fast track facts!

From racing go-karts to Formula 1 cars, they all have wheels, an engine and a steering wheel. Oh yes, and a driver!

It might be that you know all there is to know of cars, from spark plugs to carburettors (phew, that's hard to say), but let's look at some fast car smart facts ...

Cars won't get far if they don't fill up with petrol, and cars can be filled up mid-race! They have to park up in a pit-stop.

Did you know that top car races start when 5 red lights have been shown and then switched off?

Racing drivers sit in a cockpit. They call it the "tub".

How hard can it be to sit in a fast car and whizz along a track? Well, it is far harder than it looks! Top drivers have to have a lot of skill and be very fit.

Racing drivers can end up lighter at the end of a race than they were at the start! They get so hot in the kit they have on, they can shed kilos.

Marshals check that no-one is harmed at race tracks. Fans cannot charge on to the track – they have to keep well back.

Marshals have flags to send signals to drivers. A green flag shows the race has started. A yellow and red flag shows a hazard is on the track (it could be slippy patches). The black check flag signals a winner.

Constructing a go-kart can be fun. If you want a racing kart with an engine, you will need adult help! Lots of kids start off playing with go-karts and end up racing them.

If you are into racing cars, you might start with the British Karting championships. Look it up on the web!

Lewis Hamilton started racing karts when he was a lad of 8. At 10, he was the British Karting champion. He was karting's world no. 1 at 15!

Hamilton's talent was spotted when he was 13 and he signed up to race for McLaren.

The 1st Formula 1 race champion in 1950 was Nino Farina, an Italian man.

No need to be a racing driver to have a flashy, fast car – you just need £175,000.00! That is what a Ferrari 612 Scaglietti will cost!

Its top speed is 199 mph, but you need a race track to go as fast as that, as the British speed limit is just 70 mph! Go faster than that and it might be a cop car speeding to catch you up ...

Stay cool in school!

Want to be cool in school? Just follow the top tips from Nerdy Norris, the coolest kid at Kitty Kool's School for Swots and Drips.

Cool with teachers

Stand in the car park every morning to meet Miss Fobby, to help carry her books to class for her. If Big Bad Boris Briggs gets in your way, just say:

Back off Boris,
teacher's pet needs to get past!

No problem-o!

Put up your hand to tell Mr Thorn it was Crazy Charly Chugg that blocked the loo with Nora's pink tights and left a pool of wet on the floor.

When the Head, Mr Gore, tells a boring story in assembly, let your head droop and just drop off to sleep! Even more cool:

a) snore to the max

b) let drool drip on your chin.

Tell Mr Gordon, the sports teacher, that it's much too cold for rugby, so let's do the cool thing – stay in and play … chess!

If you must do PE, tell him that you tore your shorts last night, and ask if it's OK to borrow your sister's spotty pink shorts to play rugby in. When the lesson ends, spray your armpits with your sister's stinky "Lush Doll" spray. Mmmm! Dig that cool pong!

Cool with the girls

Go up to Flora Ford before school, when she's standing with her pals. Put a big box of chocs in her hands and plant a big wet kiss on her cheek.

To be even more cool, you can say:

Right at the end of the school disco, just before the lights go up, get the DJ to play a smoochy song and say:

Cool with the lads

Forget footy, Tag or Bulldog at play.

Cool kids:

- sharpen pencils for Miss Fobby
- stay in and do spellings, to get top marks in the test in the next lesson. Top of the class! Yesss!!!

Ask if you can sit next to Hard Harry Horton for story time, then weep buckets as Miss Stork gets to the sad bit at the end, when Cora Candy's pet horse gets sick. Ask Harry if you can borrow his hanky.

Nerdy says:

Why be a fool?
When in school,
To be Kid Cool,
Just follow Nerdy's top tips.

High heels - or string vests? (igh)

Green words: *Say the sounds. Say the word.*

Bright high flight right knight Wright slight light night

Say the syllables. Say the word.

Wight'man → Wightman light'ning → lightning high'ness → highness

Say the root word. Say the whole word.

swim → swimming

Red words:

of there all your call small they any to who no* me*

Challenge words:

one gross ball old gold baby lobster passengers like very lady frilly scruffy teddy lucky fluffy strappy frightfully

Vocabulary check: **MP3 player** *a small machine that stores and plays your favourite music*

mighty *big and strong* **missus** *Mrs or wife*

Know your fright limit (ow)

Green words: *Say the sounds. Say the word.*

know own show throw mow rows fright light

Say the syllables. Say the word.

shad'ow → shadow tom'o'rr ow → tomorr ow wind'ow → window

bung'a'low → bungalow

Say the root word. Say the whole word.

grow → growing

Red words:

your you what to do of who are was where so* she* my* by*

Challenge words:

don't true eyes one science wall or for hall old okay hello

Vocabulary check: **yellow belly** *someone who is easily scared*

* *These words are red for a while*

Do you do zoos? (oo)

Green words: *Say the sounds. Say the word.*

zoo food cool Jools soon choose roof

Say the syllables. Say the word.

ba'boon → baboon trop'i'cal → tropical

Say the root word. Say the whole word.

groom → grooming troop → trooping mat → matted

Red words:

you does do are they what was who there be* go* she* he* no*

Challenge words:

world their forest fur grey kangaroo brilliant or after keeper orang-utan

Vocabulary check: **pelt** *fast falling rain*

captivity *living in a small space, unable to get out* **extinct** *no longer exists*

Fast track facts (ar)

Green words: *Say the sounds. Say the word.*

park smart far kart car spark start hard

Say the syllables. Say the word.

haz'ard → hazard

Say the root word. Say the whole word.

harm → harmed kart → karting patch → patches fill → filled

Red words:

they all you to some of were could there what was want go* be* he*

Challenge words:

formula carburettor Lewis race Italian Scaglietti Ferrari champion signed don't won't kilo how driver one winner

Vocabulary check: **hazard** *danger*